The Art of Organizing and Tidying Up:

Declutter Your Home and Your Life

E.K. Larocque

© **Copyright 2021 - All rights reserved.**

The content contained within this book may not be reproduced, duplicated or transmitted without direct written permission from the author or the publisher.

Under no circumstances will any blame or legal responsibility be held against the publisher, or author, for any damages, reparation, or monetary loss due to the information contained within this book, either directly or indirectly.

Legal Notice:

This book is copyright protected. It is only for personal use. You cannot amend, distribute, sell, use, quote or paraphrase any part, or the content within this book, without the consent of the author or publisher.

Disclaimer Notice:

Please note the information contained within this document is for educational and entertainment purposes only. All effort has been executed to present accurate, up to date, reliable, complete information. No warranties of any kind are declared or implied. Readers acknowledge that the author is not engaged in the rendering of legal, financial, medical or professional advice. The content within this book has been derived from various sources. Please consult a licensed professional before attempting any techniques outlined in this book.

By reading this document, the reader agrees that under no circumstances is the author responsible for any losses, direct or indirect, that are incurred as a result of the use of the information contained within this document, including, but not limited to, errors, omissions, or inaccuracies.

Table of Contents

PREFACE 1
INTRODUCTION 3
CHAPTER 1: IT'S ALL ABOUT STUFF 7
   BENEFITS OF DECLUTTERING YOUR HOME 12
      Clear Focus *12*
      Hunting for Stuff Will Disappear *13*
      Living Spaces are Easier to Clean *13*
      Simplify *13*
      The Desire to Accumulate Unnecessary Stuff Will Diminish *13*
      Untethered *13*
      Visual Appeal *14*
   DISADVANTAGES OF DECLUTTERING 14
      Addictive *14*
      Going Too Far *14*
      It Takes Willpower *15*
      Too Much Time *15*
      You Must Be Disciplined *15*

CHAPTER 2: BECOMING MOTIVATED 16
   WHAT CAUSES CLUTTER? 20
   HOW DO YOU WANT TO FEEL? 22

CHAPTER 3: SCALING DOWN 25
   GETTING RID OF EXCESS CLUTTER 25
      Keep *26*
      Throw Away *26*
      Give Away *26*
      Sell *26*
      Uncertain *26*
   DECLUTTERING PAPER 27

Continuing with Paper...28
   Paper Serviettes...*28*
Where do I begin?..28
Finding Your Starting Point..29
   Sitting Room..*29*
   Kitchen...*32*
   Entrance Hall..*37*

CHAPTER 4: SCALING DOWN CONTINUED… 39
   Dining Room..*39*
   Bathrooms..*40*
   Bedrooms..*41*
   Hanging Closets..*44*
   Trunks and Additional Storage...*45*
   Children's Bedrooms...*46*

CHAPTER 5: THE DECLUTTERING PROCESS.................... 47
Small Steps Equal Giant Strides 47
Be Realistic..49
Take Time to Mourn 50
Handling Your Emotions Professionally 51
   Start with What You See..*51*
What Prevents Us from Achieving Our Goals? 53
Reward Yourself 54

CHAPTER 6: LIVING WITH LESS IS LIVING MORE........ 55
Having Less Means Having a Lot Less:................................55
   Cleaning..*55*
   Clean as You Go..*56*
   Debt...*56*
   Rearranging..*57*
   Stress...*57*
   Greater Financial Freedom...*57*
   Increased Energy..*57*
   Assess Your Home as a Visitor..*58*
   Take Some Before and After Photographs............................*58*
   Take up a 10 – 10 – 10 Challenge..*58*
   Donate Clothing You no Longer Wear..................................*58*

Enlist the Help of Others...*59*
Fill a Trash Bag for Goodwill..*59*
Just One Item Daily...*59*
Start Off Small..*59*
Work According to a To Do List...*59*
Stick with It..*60*
Make This an On-going Habit..*60*
Keeping Clutter Under Control..*60*
Set Up Your Systems...*61*
Refine Over Time and Streamline Even Further..*61*
Slow and Steady Progress..*62*
Procrastination...*63*
Keeping Motivated..*63*
Repurposing Storage Containers..*64*
Persevere Through the Pain..*65*

CONCLUSION... **66**

Preface

Some have asked me why it was so important to me to write this book. People tend to be surprised when I tell them the reason: I grew up in a "Hoarder House." My mother was a hoarder. She still is. I grew up with having nothing but a little passage from the door to my bed, and not always having access to my full bed. We weren't allowed to have people over, for fear of being judged, or worse, someone making a call to CPS and having me removed from the home.

At a young age, I knew that the way we lived was not normal. I would always go to my friends' houses and theirs were always normal and clean. By the time I was in High School, I had to get creative with my reasons why no one could ever come over, why the school projects needed to be done elsewhere, even though I lived closest to school. I had to be quick to find a reason when a friend's parent would drop me off and want to come in and meet my mother.

I was never a good liar, but this forced me to be. The situation forced me to be quick on my feet. As I got older, and longed to move out on my own, I was afraid that I would repeat the pattern. I had never learned any housekeeping skills; I didn't know how to cook, clean, or do most basic things. When I got my first apartment, it was basically empty, so it was quite easy to keep clean. I was so determined not to go back to the nightmare of my childhood; it was always on my mind.

I took it into my own hands by learning. I've never been of the mindset that, "If I don't know something, then I'll suffer or give up." I've always felt that if you don't know something, it's never too late to learn. This is how I learned to cook! I Googled and YouTubed, and now I'm a pretty good chef, if I do say so myself. I've failed quite a few times, but don't let that stop you from learning and getting better. If I can learn how to cook from the internet, I have no doubt that you can learn to declutter and organize with this book. You make the decision to create a clean space every day. Like all good things, it might be hard and scary to do at first. Believe in yourself, and put in the work to change your life.

Currently, I'm well in my thirties. I'm a mom and a wife; I have a full-time job. My home has become the house where everyone is always coming over or popping by. That doesn't mean that my house is 100% clean 100% of the time, being the mom to a toddler and pregnant with number two, it's not realistic to expect that of myself. Still, I look around and am shocked by what my life has turned into. Not only do I have a normal house, but I know that I broke the cycle. My daughter and baby bean won't have to live through having a hoarder parent. They can have their friends over any time they want! Playdates and birthday parties galore! You can do it, too.

Introduction

> *"In the never-ending battle between order and chaos, clutter sides with chaos every time. Anything that you possess that does not add to your life or your happiness eventually becomes a burden."*
> *– John Robbins (The New Good Life: Living better than ever in an age of less).*

Are you feeling physically drained and tired of all the stuff that seems to have accumulated around you over time and is threatening your very existence? Are you tired of spending most of your spare time tidying and dusting, and clearing away? Whenever someone announces that they're dropping by for a quick visit do you need to put them off for an hour or so while you arrange for things to be hidden away out of sight because you're just too embarrassed by the way your home looks?

If you have answered 'yes' to any of the above questions then you've probably been drawn toward this book for a very good reason. I'm going to take you on a journey where you can possibly even use a checklist to mark each of the characteristics that we will go through and discuss if you are possibly a habitual hoarder or maybe you believe in retail therapy.

For others it's the inability to either give up a bargain or having to be in vogue with the change of season, color trends, or even being fashionable. The problem with all of this is not so much in wanting all these beautiful things around your home so much as being able to know when enough is enough and being able to apply the brakes to spending habits purely because you have excess.

In *The art of organizing and tidying up: declutter your home and your life* we are going to investigate some of the long-term psychological effects of living in a state of constant clutter. How this affects the brain and ways to begin eliminating these potentially harmful habits as a matter of urgency. The good news is that you can do it. Not only when you know what you need to be doing, but also once you understand the reasoning behind it.

Are you currently living in any of the following scenarios?

- You have suitcases or boxes with clothing, shoes, handbags, toys, books, or anything else you could conceivably think of that you haven't used or looked at for the last 6 to 12 months?
- You have to open cupboards or drawers extra cautiously because you're not sure what's likely to fall out of the drawers.
- You have papers everywhere that are out of order—examples of these could be bank statements, utility bills, clothing accounts, school reports.
- You are hanging onto items of clothing from four or five seasons ago, "just in case" you are able to lose enough weight to fit into them someday.
- You feel claustrophobic with all the stuff surrounding you.
- You often spend unnecessary time looking for keys, glasses, cell phones, remote controls because you simply cannot remember where you put them.

We are going to consider ways that you can keep all those things that still have meaning for you, while sorting and sifting through things that are broken, no longer being used, or that you may no longer have a need for.

In the course of the chapters that follow we will discuss motivation to actually begin this process and how to push through whenever you feel the pressure becoming too much for you to bear. Being successful in organizing and tidying up is part of keeping your life on track. Once you begin to notice the benefits of becoming more organized this will assist you when it comes to motivation.

However, there is also a bit of a warning when taking on a project of this size and magnitude. You need to be realistic with what you will be able to manage at any given time. Try not to tackle an insurmountable task within an unreasonable time frame. All that this will do will set you up for feeling completely overwhelmed and unable to manage some of even the simplest of tasks.

As we go through The art of organizing and tidying up: declutter your home and your life there will be certain tips, hacks, and ideas for you to choose from. Just as with everything in life, the beauty of advice is that it's something that is very unique and individual. There may be certain techniques that work especially well for you, while others may not. I urge you to look for those techniques that are going to add value to your home and your life.

As you manage to work your way through each of the following chapters, you will begin to feel your life becoming simpler and unburdened by all the stuff of the world that we often become bogged down with. Once you have managed to work through your initial spaces and regained control over your life, the next secret is being able to maintain it.

Keeping clutter under control is going to take discipline, time, and patience. Unfortunately, as much as we would like to be able to wave a magic wand and have the declutter and organization fairies pay us a visit, it's never going to happen. Whatever we want to achieve we are going to have to work on these constantly.

The main aim when working to regain control of the chaos that seems to have engulfed our lives, we need to be patient enough for it to become a habit.

Developing habits that are firmly ingrained in ourselves to the point where we can implement them at a moment's notice is what we are aiming for. It's getting to the point where you have sufficient special awareness that you can immediately pick up when there is, or when there is likely to be clutter challenges.

We will discuss things like repurposing containers or things that really mean something to you. After all, what is the point of having something that you love and you don't get to enjoy it because it's tucked away in a cupboard somewhere?

The main aim with *The art of organizing and tidying up: declutter your home and your life* is helping you to create long-lasting habits that can simply be kicked into high gear as soon as you need them. It is also having the discipline to be able to check yourself and recognize when things are becoming too much to handle.

There are multiple benefits of developing the habit of keeping your environment organized and tidy. It can help you eliminate stress that you may be feeling at the time. In most instances, the stress is brought on by being surrounded by chaos and mayhem.

Finally, one of the ultimate, most important benefits that can be enjoyed as soon as you manage to succeed at developing this habit is not only a better, more comfortable, spacious, and organized environment. But it will also have a positive effect on the mental health and general well-being of all within the home.

If you've felt that you've been physically drawn to this book for whatever reason, then there's possibly a message in the pages that follow. You may be drawn to certain chapters more than others; this is possibly because there's a lesson for you in that section. Other chapters may need to be read and reread for maximum benefit. One of the most important benefits is that through small and simple daily actions, great change can emerge.

Chapter 1:

It's All About Stuff

"Clutter is not just physical stuff, it's old ideas, toxic relationships and bad habits."
– Eleanor Brown

If you're anything like I was in the past you have probably been collecting a lot of stuff along the way and this occasionally overwhelms you. The visual reminder of materialistic belongings building up and taking up every open space that you are trying to live in can begin to weigh heavily on your mental health and may even begin to cause you to feel some anxiety.

This is caused by all the stuff we've decided to attach to our lives. The big question we need to be asking ourselves however is, what is the reasoning behind our need to have so many things? Do we fear that we will someday lose out on something by not owning so many belongings? Or are we simply trying to keep us with those we socialize with?

When we consider all of our belongings or stuff, what value are we attaching to our lives as we begin to hang onto each of these items? Do we understand the reason behind why we are choosing to do this? One of the most important things we need to identify before we can even begin to declutter and tidy our environments is to discover why we feel the need to do this in the first instance.

If you don't have a clear understanding of why you want to do this then you simply won't stick to it, which is the main objective of trying to simplify your life. You want to be in the right frame of mind before you even begin this type of project. Right off the bat I'm going to tell you that this will not be something you will accomplish overnight, and it is not something you will only do once.

From the moment you begin to simplify your life by getting rid of all those items that no longer serve you, you will begin to feel lighter, as if a weight has been lifted from your shoulders and those things you are going to choose to hang on to will only be things that actually serve a purpose and add value to who you are as an individual or as a family.

One of the first things you will probably need to do is discover the reason for why you have so much stuff to begin with. Are you a compulsive shopper or someone who thrives on retail therapy? Do things like fashion and seasonal trends influence you? An example of this could be different tones and textures that happen to come into fashion for a season and you automatically just have to make changes to your living room area, bedrooms, bathrooms, or other areas in your home.

Are you a compulsive hoarder? Possibly you grew up in a time where certain things were scarce and as an adult you are now afraid of having to relive this experience all over again. All that this has done has caused you to become way more paranoid over owning more and more stuff.

If you have ever found yourself looking around you and being completely bombarded with belongings but you're too afraid to let anything go just in case you might need it further down the line. This is another major problem and can be closely linked to the hoarding association. You probably don't even need a fraction of what you have, but it makes you feel good about yourself knowing that you have what you want around you.

Maybe you come from a home or family where things were constantly changing, the furniture and furnishings were being rearranged on a regular basis to accommodate the sheer volume of stuff that you own. If you happen to be living in a home where you cannot open a cupboard door without having things jump out at you or fall out because there is so much chaos and excess then you really are in trouble and that's the main purpose behind this book.

Something you're going to have to own up to is what is your thought process behind having all of these belongings. There has to be one. You may need to analyze this and reanalyze this over and over again to get down to the real reason why you feel you need to be hanging onto everything that you are. One of the biggest reasons for people enduring clutter and too many things is because they grew up in an environment of poverty. They are terrified of ever having to move back into this space once more, so rather having too much seems so much better to them than cutting back and being forced to decide what you really need. Necessity as a starting point can be a good thing but reaching the decision needs to be something you're really comfortable with.

The next step is identifying that you may have a problem to begin with. That you don't need five or six pairs of boots where one or two will do. You don't need to have clothes shoved in your wardrobe that you know you are never going to be able to fit into ever again. There's no value in holding onto items that are broken, just in case at some stage you may need them. The sensible thing to do when faced with this situation is to get rid of things immediately if they are broken.

Are you used to wasting hours and hours of precious time looking for things that could quite easily be tidied up, placed in one place, where clutter can be eliminated, making these items easier for everyone to find? Would living in clean, clear, minimalist spaces not make things a whole lot easier for you? How much time are you spending cleaning and tidying up that could be better spent with family, friends, or loved ones?

Psychologically, when you have too much going on around you when it comes to clutter, this can cause mental confusion and overload as well. All that you see wherever you look is too much stuff piled high with little to no order. It is enough to make one stressed out with the condition of things and even creating sufficient anxiety for you to not be able to focus on getting those things done that you need to do.

Let's face it, cleaning and tidying takes up time, effort, and loads of energy. Under normal circumstances a cluttered home takes much longer to clean than one that is minimalist and organized. The reason for this is very often all you end up doing with the cluttered environment is shuffling the clutter from one place to the next.

The only way to begin to get this under control is to look for ways to start making inroads and changes to your current lifestyle so you can regain control of your life. It actually has very little to do with the amount of stuff that you have and more to do with what you have and the amount of joy and happiness that this brings into your life at any given moment.

Before moving onto the following chapters and discovering how important this is to you in your life. You need to make a firm commitment that you really want to change your current way of life. Part of this is also identifying your main reason for wanting to change:

- Are you tired of cleaning?
- Do you want to live longer?
- Are you wanting to spend quality time with your loved ones?

- Do you want to cut back on the volume of stuff you have?
- Do your belongings really bring you joy and happiness?
- Do you want to save yourself time?
- Are you looking to create harmony in the home?

Each of these is valuable reasons for wanting to jump in and begin organizing your home by clearing away the clutter. Beginning today, you must be willing to commit to this process 100%. If you have any doubts whatsoever this will result in you not following through with the process. One of the other main things worth mentioning right at the beginning of this book is that it is going to take you quite a while to begin to see results. You are doing this as part of a lifestyle change.

You want to be able to develop sound and solid habits that you can learn to stick with. These are values and habits that you can also teach your children if you have any. The benefits are not just for you, but they are for all who enter your home. There will be less fighting and contention over not being able to find certain important things, there will also be less stuff to have to monitor and keep tidy.

Making this life-altering decision is something definitely not to be entered into lightly. You want everyone in the home to be happy with the decision. Explaining the pros and cons to them may help making this decision become easier for them to do. Part of this process is being able to survive with less than what you currently have by cutting back, thinning the fat so to speak and then living your very best life moving forward.

Recognize that having all the clutter around you day in and day out is emotionally and physically draining. You may not even realize that the clutter around you is influencing you in a negative way. Believe me when I tell you that it is though. Another part of getting rid of all those things that are taking up space, yet they aren't bringing true value or joy to your life is that they are preventing you from living your life intentionally.

Do you believe that you can change the trajectory of your life simply by decluttering and organizing your home and your life? It may sound like it's a bit of a stretch and virtually impossible to do, and when you initially begin it will honestly feel like you have taken on way more than you can handle, yet at the same time, after a short while of getting rid of all those things you don't want, you will begin to recognize the intentional life coming to the forefront of your new lifestyle. It's a question of becoming intentional with everything that you decide to hold onto, rather than just keeping things out of necessity or wanting them because they make you feel more secure within yourself.

Benefits of Decluttering Your Home

Seven ways to help you live an intentional life are as follows:

Clear Focus

You will be able to focus on those things that are really important to you and your life because you are no longer focusing on clutter all around you. Mentally and psychologically the brain activates on visual stimulus, therefore everything that happens to be around you all day long will become part of the distraction that your brain is just looking for. Without being able to clear away these distractions, the clutter will continue having its negative control over your brain. This will also dictate where your thoughts go whenever you come across chaos in the home or even in your office. Becoming organized means becoming more efficient and effective wherever you would prefer to focus your energy. It becomes easier to focus more fully in an environment that is simpler, neater, and cleaner.

Hunting for Stuff Will Disappear

The endless circling around and around searching for critical items, especially when you need them at the last minute can be enough to drive anyone crazy. There's no bigger frustration than frantically having to search for your car keys because you need to be at a meeting within a short space of time. You know that you saw them somewhere, but where? All of this dancing back and forth looking for anything that's important and time sensitive can lead to feelings of being totally out of control.

Living Spaces are Easier to Clean

Imagine how much easier areas will be able to clean and keep clean once they have been given a complete makeover with organization and decluttering. Instead of wasting hours having to move items to dust behind them or dust beside them, everything will now have its own special place.

Simplify

This is possibly one of the greatest benefits you will experience with this entire exercise. Your life will become much simpler. You will be able to finally live with purpose and intentionally without being a slave to the things you own.

The Desire to Accumulate Unnecessary Stuff Will Diminish

Having gone through a thorough decluttering experience, you should begin to realize that you don't actually need to be a compulsive shopper to own nice things and be happy. You can actually accomplish this by finding joy in each of the items you currently possess, or those items you have chosen to hang onto.

Untethered

Too much stuff can actually weigh you down, making you feel like a ship that's been anchored far out at sea. As you begin to declutter your life and your home you will begin to feel lighter emotionally as though the anchor is no longer there, and the rest of your life is going to be smooth sailing.

Visual Appeal

We know how unsightly clutter can be. Whether it's dishes piled high in the washbasin or laundry waiting to be folded. Constantly being visually reminded of things that need to be done can sidetrack us from exactly where our attention should be focused. On the other hand, when we are looking at clean, crisp, clear, open spaces, mentally we can direct our thoughts to wherever they may be required.

Disadvantages of Decluttering

We happened to mention that these were some of the benefits of clearing away the clutter that seems to be engulfing and swallowing up every nook and cranny in your home. What are some of the disadvantages though?

Addictive

Going this route can become so cathartic that it actually becomes a form of addiction. This is bad for you because instead of doing those things that you really want to be doing in life you are now totally engrossed with keeping all your stuff down to the bare minimum. This is not what it is all about because this will leave you feeling hard done by. The most important thing about following this lifestyle is keeping everything aligned and harmonious and balanced.

Going Too Far

Very similar to above, but this is taking things to the extreme where you cut your possessions right down to the very bare essentials. This is not the point of decluttering. It is not meant to leave you feeling depressed because you now have so few belongings that you are feeling dissatisfied with your life at the moment.

It Takes Willpower

You will need to monitor yourself constantly to be sure that you are not slipping back into old habits. Developing willpower is something that happens gradually over time and is not something that you can automatically acquire.

Too Much Time

A huge factor when it comes to this is that you will have a lot more time on your hands. You aren't going to spend a fraction of the time sorting and trying to work things out as you get into a routine. Choosing what to do with your excess time is something that's important. You could easily make all the wrong decisions and instead of spending quality time with loved ones you can get sucked into playing computer games or becoming involved with other things that are counterproductive rather than valuable.

You Must Be Disciplined

To master this lifestyle change you need to become disciplined but balanced at the same time. This means being mentally astute when it comes to decision-making. Rather than verging on cutting things right down, be sure that you are still comfortable in your decisions. Work toward creating a sense of harmony and balance in all things.

Chapter 2:

Becoming Motivated

"You'll never change your life until you change something you do daily. The secret of your success is found in your daily routine."
– John C. Maxwell

In chapter 1 we discussed how you won't be very effective at implementing major changes in your life and your home until you decide for yourself that it's what you want to do. It doesn't help to try to declutter your life, your home, and anywhere else on the basis that it's actually someone else's decision or choice for your life. All that this will do will make you totally frustrated.

Chances are you may begin the process, but it will end up being something that is half-hearted, and you will probably throw in the towel at the very first sign of challenges or obstacles. This is one of the last things that you really want to be doing when it comes to this life-altering experience. Before you even begin to think about decluttering and reorganizing your space, you need to discover what the motivation is behind what you want to do.

The big question is why do you want to change? If when you answer this question you are answering that it's the decision of another member of your family, unless you are 100% totally committed to the process, don't even go there. Wait until the decision or choice to make a lifestyle change becomes your own. Once this decision is going to be made with you and your loved ones in mind, your motivation becomes worthwhile and sustainable.

Identify several reasons why you want to make these changes to your life right now. That way, each of these reasons will be what will keep you motivated to get the momentum going. They will help you when you feel like giving in, when things become tough, when you have difficult choices to make, and these will come, or when you are just plain tired of cleaning and sorting, and trying to make your home a calmer, more inviting place to live in.

If you aren't sure how to get your momentum going, think about how the present state of clutter is making you feel? Chances are, just by looking at it, you are already feeling physically drained and tired? You know that you've accumulated too much stuff when it's starting to take up every single nook and cranny. Where shelves are full, and drawers or cupboards are filled to capacity, but you aren't even sure what's in half of these places.

Is all of the chaos surrounding you making you feel anxious or depressed? Did you even realize that this is possible? By having too many things that are disorganized all over the place, your mind is often naturally drawn toward these places. Chances are that they also seem to completely overwhelm you, rather than bringing you the happiness, peace, and joy that you should be getting from absolutely everything that you choose to have in your home.

Here are some of the most important reasons for you to think about when you're planning on doing a major clean out, decluttering, and reorganizing operation.

It can provide you with the opportunity to reduce your stress levels. Just making the decision to begin a project of this magnitude will help you feel as though you are once more taking control of your life and everything in it. This is instead of allowing your belongings to determine what you do. Your mental health will also improve as you finally make these decisions because once again, you are not allowing all your materialistic 'stuff' to dictate to you, or to feel constantly pressurized by living under cramped conditions.

Finding a place for things, can make it easier to find when you really need them can help you feel less stressed because you won't be panicking or wasting valuable time trying to find things. Getting rid of clutter is more than just packing away, it's a means of simplifying your life and helping you offload a lot of things that are causing you stress.

The world we live in is constantly bombarding us with all sorts of demands and challenges. We only add to all this stress by not getting our personal behavior under control. The behavior that I'm referring to is that of either not tidying up after yourself or living with too many belongings. Clutter only adds to emotions of chaos.

Are you genuinely happy as you are now? Does everything within your home bring you joy? Do you dread walking into your home at the end of a day at the office because you know there's too much to do and there just don't seem to be enough hours in a day?

Chaos and clutter can really cause us to feel stressed out. This is one of the reasons why minimalism is suddenly becoming extremely popular once again. People are working with these as tools in the wellness industry.

Let's look at some of the benefits that you could experience if you choose to declutter your home or office space:

One of the most important things that it gives you is renewed control over your space. Once everything has been safely secured or put away where it belongs or there have now been designated areas designed for these belongings, you don't need to feel so out of control anymore. It means that whenever you're looking for something you know exactly where to find it. Something that should be just as important to mention here though is that when you make use of something, to keep your environment in the same standard of order and cleanliness, you need to put things back where you have found them.

Getting rid of things that you really don't need relieves you of tremendous pressure. Imagine that your entire garage is full of boxes, storage bins, and old suitcases. You keep going through them over and over again, like someone who is ruminating. You battle to label each container correctly because no sooner do you do so when someone else is rummaging through them and things don't get returned to where they belong.

Amongst these bins, boxes, and cases you have old clothes, shoes, hats, broken handbags, CDs and DVDs that are scratched beyond redemption. You have linen that you haven't used in the last 5 years, maybe even some of the clothes fall into this category. There's wrapping paper that's so dusty and torn that you're not entirely sure whether you'll ever be able to use it again.

Every time you even think about entering the garage, you become too spooked because the amount of work that's there to be done just seems to overwhelm you. There's really no sense of urgency to getting it sorted out just yet, so you leave the garage door closed for as long as you can. Because there is so much 'stuff' that's been accumulated you can no longer fit your car into the garage where it belongs, and it is getting damaged by the elements.

You still don't have a sense of urgency to do too much about it. Now, imagine the exact same scenario where you've decided to sell your home. You need to get everything sorted out for people to view the house and be interested in putting in an offer. Any real estate agent worth their salt will tell you that a home that is too cluttered will battle to find a buyer because buyers cannot imagine themselves living in the space (mainly because there doesn't appear to be any).

The day will finally come when you are absolutely forced to make a decision regarding what you have stored away. Some of the items will have sentimental value, while other items are disposable, and you wouldn't miss them if they were to be dealt with appropriately. As you begin to work through each of these items you will feel a tremendous sense of empowerment returning to you. It will no longer be the clutter that will decide or dictate to you what your home is going to look like.

Clutter actually interferes with our ability to focus correctly. It has the power to disrupt or break our concentration, it may even pull us away from doing the things we need to be doing in order to do something else. This could interfere with how productive we are throughout the day. According to a study published in *Current Psychology in 2017* apart from the decrease in productivity, there was a marked increase in the level of procrastination taking place.

What Causes Clutter?

The simple answer to this question is when we have too many belongings that we are attached to. It's having too many possessions. Many individuals mistakenly believe that the more you have the wealthier you actually are. This is not entirely true. You can be an expert at bargain hunting, paying very little for all your 'possessions' only to have them make you feel miserable. It is not directly linked to how much money you have in the bank.

The number of possessions you happen to own could also be a result of your upbringing where you were raised during part of the war, the great depression, if you have survived recessions, or even your very own personal financial setback. You may have had to go without for a while. This has created a shopaholic individual who needs their regular retail therapy fix. It really doesn't matter what is being purchased, as long as you are constantly able to add to the possessions.

Being able to live a life of abundance in itself is not a problem but we should also know how to temper this emotion. Everything should be evenly balanced for us to live a full and happy life.

What about working in a cluttered environment? This was definitely something I was particularly bad at because I hated filing. The problem with being in an office that has papers piled high is that eventually something is going to fall through the cracks and it's going to be your head on the line. You need to find that happy balance, or at least become totally organized so that you know where everything is.

Part of the secret to decluttering and organizing your space is making sure that you have everything that you need at your disposal and you know where everything is. I would probably spend more time trying to sort out my office several times a year than what it would have taken me to do a little bit every day, or to at least keep the piles in my inbox and outbox under control.

When you procrastinate in an office environment this can easily influence and impact your decision-making ability.

Another negative way that clutter can impact your life is by causing a hazardous environment. Too many papers, boxes, and other paraphernalia lying around can potentially be a slip and fall hazard if one has to navigate around them, or if they are too close to electrical cables, this can prove to be a fire hazard.

Another negative aspect comes in when it comes to having way too much clutter around you is that it could set off differences of opinion in relationships. If you and your partner have different ideas when it comes to things being neat and tidy or even just orderly, and you can't keep your environment under control, this is going to bring disharmony into the home.

If you are too embarrassed by what your home looks like because of all the clutter, this could result in you no longer socializing with others purely out of shame.

There's nothing positive about having too much clutter around you. If you have ever heard of Mari Kondo her philosophy on organizing and decluttering spaces may come across to some as being completely radical, but what she does believe in that is a valuable lesson for us all when trying to navigate through this maze of clutter that we've been holding onto for such a long time is that whatever you decide to keep should bring you joy.

Once again, my level of joy, or those things that will bring me joy versus those things that are going to bring you joy in this life may be completely different. This is her only criteria. If it holds a special place in your heart and you really feel that you need it in your life and in your space, then feel free to hang onto it.

How Do You Want to Feel?

The various emotions you feel at any given time can either positively or negatively affect not only your life but also the lives of those around you. Now that we've discussed how your current situation is making you feel about yourself and your life it's time for you to decide how you want to feel instead. The ideal emotions you're looking for are ones that are going to make you happy. You want to feel lighter inside, rather than under emotional pressure. You are looking for those emotions that are going to make you want to keep moving toward the life of your dreams. What will this look like?

- Would you like to feel liberated and free from all the clutter?
- Do you want to feel peace, joy and contentment every time you look around you?

- Are you wanting to spend more quality time with family and loved ones without having to waste it needlessly cleaning constantly?
- Are there things that you could be doing now that could begin to make these changes happen in your life?
- How accomplished will you feel if you manage to pull this off and then stick with it?

These are all vital questions and the answers are contained in several of the chapters that follow as a step-by-step guide is going to show you exactly what you need to be doing and how you can possibly even make use of several life hacks to make the decluttering process easier for you. It is still definitely going to take a lot of hard work, but it should be something to look forward to.

Too often there are questions being asked as to how much clutter is an acceptable norm, and when does it become a problem. I would argue that the moment you realize that some of your space is beginning to look cluttered, that's when it's got to be sorted out and get out of your way. Something that should be understood when it comes to clutter is that it can easily take over your life if you let it. Once you start this decluttering and reorganizing project, it needs to become part of your lifestyle.

This is not a once-off thing. Unfortunately for us we are consumers and as consumers there will always be packets and boxes, bags, and paper that we deal with daily. This is anything from the cartons our milk comes into the paper bags you receive doing shopping. Something has to happen with each of these things to prevent them from accumulating and once again taking over your life.

We continue to receive mail, even in this digital age. There are still a limited number of broadsheets or newspapers still being printed. In many areas these contain the local news and happenings in the community. Despite the fact that these may only be delivered once a week, when you consider the number of pages each newspaper has and multiply this by the number of weeks in a year, you will have a stack of paper if you aren't recycling.

Mental health practitioners are associating clutter with stress, anxiety, and depression. Because clutter is so visual, you really cannot do too much about hiding it from yourself and certain things are a constant reminder of what needs to be done. Just as clutter is linked with various mental health issues, resolving clutter can actually help you learn to relax, regain perspective, begin to feel a sense of accomplishment in your life once more, and remove feelings of guilt, shame, and being overwhelmed.

There can be a downside to decluttering spaces and that's when it virtually becomes an obsession. When you become so strict on yourself that you don't allow yourself some of life's greatest opportunities—living your very best life without putting yourself down all the time. Remember that the secret to this entire process is benefiting yourself and keeping your life in a state of balance and harmony.

In the chapters that follow we are going to look at ways that you can begin doing this so that it cuts out most of the sensations of being completely overwhelmed by the chaos.

Chapter 3:

Scaling Down

"Having more and more won't solve the problem, and happiness does not lie in possessions or even relationships. The answer lies within ourselves. If we can't find peace and happiness there, it's not going to come from the outside."
– Tenzin Palmo

In this chapter we are going to look at how to scale down and trim back the fat so to speak. There are some proven methods that work really well in getting you to the point where you can seriously begin to reorganize your home. In the meantime however, let's look at ways that you can scale down on some of your possessions and take the first few steps when it comes to tidying up.

Getting Rid of Excess Clutter

Before we dive into getting rid of excess clutter, here's what you need to know about the main method we are planning on using. We will refer to this as the five-pile sorting method, and it's going to be used throughout your decluttering process:

Keep

These are items that have real meaning for you in your life and you can simply not do without these items.

Throw Away

You definitely know that you don't need to be hanging onto this anymore. It adds no value to your life, if anything it detracts from your life and seems to be weighing you down. This is often visual clutter and is usually those items we have in abundance or excess.

Give Away

Items that you know are still in a good condition that someone else may get good use out of them. You are not planning on entering into a financial negotiation with these items. They are a gift that is freely given with love.

Sell

These are items that are still in really good condition that you have possibly hardly used, or they are still brand new. These items can often be advertised for sale or to swap for something else. Once you complete your clearing exercise you may just be surprised by how much money you are able to get by selling off those items you really have no use for.

Uncertain

These are items that hold both value and sentimentality to you yet you aren't entirely sure whether you're in a place to let them go or whether you need some extra time to decide. It's quite fine for you to be feeling this way regarding your possessions, let's face it, often we have had to work extremely hard to be able to afford each of the things that we have collected along life's journey so far.

Being armed with each of these five steps it's now a chance to begin the decluttering process in earnest.

Decluttering Paper

One of the first steps of getting rid of excess clutter is by starting with unnecessary paper. In almost every household there always seems to be a favorite drawer somewhere or cupboard where all the excess paper and old documents end up. This is the very first place you need to be using as a starting point.

Literally go through every piece of paper and sort them out by date. Anything older than 5 years old can quite comfortably be thrown away. You are going to want to keep all documents that have any legal implications. These will be things like bank statements, lease agreements for property documents. This doesn't matter whether they relate to fixed property like your home, or movable property like your motor vehicle. To keep all of these documents together and organized effectively I would recommend looking for a concertina file where documents can be sorted into different sections.

It is probably wise to keep medical bills and other expense documents that you may need for tax purposes together. These can even be filed under 'Taxes.' Separate any business and personal documents if you happen to be running your own business. Especially if that business is being run remotely from home. You will have tax implications that may be important when it comes to submitting your tax information. This may differ from state to state, but your tax consultant will be able to assist you with this advice.

You may be holding onto each of your children's artwork from when they were in kindergarten. While each of these items may be cute to look at they will begin to fade over time and become destroyed. One of the ways to preserve these memories is to take photographs that can be printed and scrapbooked or placed in other journals or photo albums for you to refer back to as and when you want. There you are considering one album rather than hoarding mountains of different shapes, painted handprints, holiday cards and other letters from your children. Thankfully we live in a digital age and it's easy enough to be able to scan each of these things onto an external drive where you have access to them whenever you feel that you want to reminisce.

Continuing with Paper

Other documents or bits of paper that may seem to be overwhelming you and swallowing you whole are things like gift wrap, gift bags that you may have received gifts in. There is no reason for you to hang onto any of these items. Unless you are able to guarantee that the paper is still going to be in a good condition for the following season, or can be repurposed, get rid of it.

Paper Serviettes

There's a strong possibility that you went out to purchase very specific serviettes for Halloween, Thanksgiving, Hanukkah, Christmas, and so the various celebrations continue. There always seem to be a couple of serviettes left. Either make use of these during normal meals when you aren't expecting guests or get rid of them.

Something few people consider as clutter is cash receipts or credit card receipts. If you are sitting with a purse or wallet full of these receipts and you have no use for them, please throw them out. If you are concerned about keeping accurate records of all your bank transactions, print out copies of your bank statements and save these in their own separate file or in your concertina file.

Once you have gone through the entire house and cleared out all the excess paperwork you should already begin to feel a whole lot lighter.

Where do I begin?

One of the reasons why people procrastinate when it comes to decluttering and organizing is because they become so overwhelmed by what has to happen that they don't know where to begin. This is nothing new and please don't let this deter you because the truth is that there's no right or wrong answer here. For me there are always two different starting points that spring to mind. I think of common areas in the home or areas that you may be inviting guests into as being some of the most important and possibly key areas to begin your decluttering exercise.

For others they prefer to start in the smallest room in the home and then work their way up to the area that seems to have the most work in it. Chances are once you get started you will find yourself close to coming up with a plan that works best for you. Don't let others tell you that you have to start in room x or room y... it's nonsense or possibly just sales hype. And yes, you may want to start in your own personal bedroom so that at the end of every day you can get into a clean, freshly cleaned, organized environment and you get to enjoy it rather than leaving this till last.

Finding Your Starting Point

If you are working together as a family on this project, allow everyone to put in their input. Discuss every single area of the home including laundries, basements, garages, garden sheds, and so on. When you go through this decluttering exercise every single item that you possess should be considered in the process. The next thing would be to arrange for a pen and paper and complete an audit on the entire contents of the space you're working with.

Write down each item as you would do if you were doing a physical stocktake of items in a store. An example of this would be:

Sitting Room
- Books x 100
- Candle holders x 6
- Candles x 8

- Coffee tables x 7
- CDs x 150
- Lamps x 6
- Magazines x 72
- Ornaments x 40
- Photo frames x 6
- Plants x 8
- Rugs x 2
- Scatter cushions x 12
- Single seaters x 2
- Sofas x 2
- Throws x 4
- Wall hangings (art) x 6

Immediately by looking at the list above you can tell that unless you have a really great bookcase, you have way too many books. Here are the questions you need to ruthlessly ask yourself:

- Have you read all of them?
- Are you likely to read all of them?
- Are there some of them that you bought on a whim and you know that you'll never read them? If so, set all of them to one side.
- Those that you have read, do you really want to keep them? If so, set them to another side that's marked with a sign "TO KEEP."

- If you are really not sure whether you would like to keep them or not, place them into another pile that's marked 'UNDECIDED.'

- Those that you know you're happy to part with, place in another pile marked "GIVE AWAY" or one of the following two piles to 'SELL' or to "THROW AWAY." This is commonly referred to as a 5-pile method of sorting.

You may find that some of your books are in excellent condition and they can be sold as used books, or, you may not have even read them and they're brand new. In this instance you may want to donate them somewhere or give them away.

This is the process that you are going to make use of throughout your home in sorting out everything that you own.

In the example we used above, something that's abundantly clear is that you also have way too many ornaments… Many of these may have once had sentimental value to you, they may have been reminders of trips to different countries, or gifts from your children when they were little and so on. In this instance, you will really have to make some tough decisions as to what you want to hold onto and what you are now prepared to let go. You may be surprised at what they are worth by doing a little research on the internet if your ornaments are specific to an era, or they happen to be unique, numbered, produced in a particular part of the world, there are often collectors out there. As in individuals that will really appreciate each piece for exactly what it is. For any single sitting room though, having all those knick-knacks is likely to send your head spinning from all the visual over stimuli.

Go back through every item on the list sorting each item into one of the five different piles.

Immediately considering our example as given above, there are too many candles that are visually present. Candles are something that you can use in different areas of the home. Consider rearranging these or moving them to different parts of the home where they can be enjoyed rather than all sitting in one place.

Having so many coffee tables in one area can also be too much visually. Even if they are small side coffee tables. Consider rearranging your sitting room, making it more functional and getting rid of excess furnishings so that it doesn't appear visually overstimulated. Sort through all of your CDs. Set aside any duplicates. Look for ones that are scratched and cannot be saved. Place these in the throw away pile.

As we do this I am going to give you some pointers of things specifically to watch out for as you go from room to room. In no particular order,

Kitchen

Decant all your small amounts of sauces such as ketchup, Ranch, and mustard into single bottles or containers and get rid of all the rest. Repeat this same process with all sauces that may be sitting in your pantry or your refrigerator. You are ideally looking for only one open bottle at a time. If you like to repurpose the glass bottles then clean them immediately and find a place to store them until you're ready to use them for something else.

Do exactly the same thing with your herbs and spices. We may notice that we're running low on say, "Italian Herbs" and so the next time we're out shopping we buy a replacement. This is where the problem comes in. Instead of decanting what's left of the old container into the new container, or vice versa, we sit with two or more open containers that have to be cleaned and cared for. If you don't have decent spice bottles, consider other empty jars, bottles, or containers that you may have laying around gathering dust that can specifically be repurposed for your spices. Some great examples of this are the glass bottles that baby food comes in, the lids are sealable and the neck is wide enough for you to be able to pinch the spices safely. You can get a fair amount of spice in each of these containers.

Sort all foodstuffs into containers rather than leaving them in their original packaging. This not only makes for space saving but easy sorting, stacking, and packing, and unpacking. Make use of sturdy containers for heavier items such as sugar, rice, and flour, while smaller containers would be better suited to things like herbs, spices and food flavoring. Normal condiments like jams and spreads should be left in their original packaging.

By the time you have done this with all your foodstuffs it's time to clean out kitchen cupboards or the pantry for storing each of these items. Pack tall containers toward the back of the cupboard or pantry for ease of access. These tall containers could contain anything from spaghetti, other pasta, breakfast cereals, rice, or flour. It would be hugely beneficial if the containers can be stacked or neatly aligned with one another and are transparent, making it easy to identify the contents. Smaller containers are great for tea, coffee, hot chocolate, spices, and smaller pasta shapes such as shells or twirls.

One of the most important things to remember when it comes to placing your foodstuffs into other containers is they must be able to seal properly. This not only protects the food from any moisture that may be in the air, but also from bugs such as ants or weevils. The whole purpose of this exercise is to keep your foodstuffs fresher for longer and organized, making cleaning a breeze, as well as being able to reach in and find exactly what you are looking for. Consider things like a proper spice rack that you can keep all your dried herbs and spices all in one place, making them easy to access, especially when cooking.

As you clean out your cupboards and your pantry get rid of anything that is past its "best before date." You should consider doing this with all your canned foods as well. Any canned foods should be stored with the oldest items in the front, with the fresher items toward the back or below. Your aim is to use up those goods before they reach their expiration date. You want to practice this with all food in your pantry.

Cleaning out your refrigerator is something that should definitely be done on a regular basis. However, if you learn how to "clean as you go" this time-consuming task can take care of itself with minimal effort. Examine all the contents in your refrigerator and toss anything that is either past its "best before date," or looks as though it's no longer fresh.

Part of this journey is to focus on hanging on to only those things that bring you joy. It's very difficult for fruit or vegetables that are wilting or beginning to lose their shape or natural coloring to bring you joy. By regularly assessing what your fresh foods look like, you can easily keep this under control. As with all the sauces and condiments, aim for only one jar of each item in the refrigerator at any given time. There's nothing worse than three of four containers of exactly the same sauce with tiny little bits in each. Either use them up, amalgamate them into one container or toss them.

Your kitchen will also more than likely have cupboard space or packing space for your dinner service or crockery and cutlery. Instead of settling for several items that don't match (unless it's intentional), choose the best of the various sets and only stick with the number of plates, side plates, and bowls you actually need. Remember that your main aim is to reduce the amount of time spent working at cleaning. The more 'stuff' you have, the more you have to clean.

By all means, keep a really good dinner service if you love entertaining. You will have a pretty good idea as to how many people you entertain at any given time. This would usually be a different dinner service to what you are using every other day. Not only should this dinner service be separated from your normal service, but it should also be taken care of because it is used for special occasions. Everything that is normally used whenever you entertain should be kept together. This could be anything from Napkins, table runners, fancy wine glasses or champagne flutes, placemats, plate holders, and possibly even candles that you would normally enjoy with a close intimate social setting. The main idea is to remove these items where they can easily become chipped or broken when used as part of your "everyday settings."

Whenever you find a chipped or broken glass, mug, or plate, either choose to repurpose it or get rid of these items. Depending on the size of your family keep one or two settings out per person and get rid of the rest. Choose the settings that really speak to your soul and bring you joy and happiness.

Repeat this same process with each of your salad bowls, soup bowls and any other containers that you may have collected over the years. As you are sorting through each item remember to ask yourself each of the following key questions:

- When did you last make use of the item?
- Is it something you can manage to live without?
- Do you really need it?
- Does it hold sentimental value to you?
- Is it something that brings you peace, harmony, and joy?
- If your house burnt down and you happen to lose everything, will this be something you will feel devastated over losing?

If you have answered 'no' to a number of the above questions it may be time to seriously rethink some of those items you're hanging onto. Are you doing it for all the right reasons, or merely because you can?

Repeat the same process with your pots and pans. I have recently replaced my set of cookware that after some 30 years had more than served their purpose. My previous, old faithful set will be handed onto someone else who just might be able to make use of them. You may be wondering how pots and pans can last as long as they have? The answer is simple, I made a very wise, expensive investment when I was extremely young. I fell for the sales talk that this cookware would last and paid a hefty price tag for them back in the day.

Needless to say, I more than received the value that I paid for this set of pots and pans. Today, I no longer have to worry about whether items are going to be easily destroyed and so the time finally arrived to replace these with something more modern. Here's part of the secret when it comes down to spending large amounts of money on anything. You can go two different routes as with anything in life—quality versus quantity. By saving a few dollars, I was able to purchase additional things like new drying cloths to match the main color scheme that I have throughout my kitchen. I still chose a more expensive set of cookware than I initially thought to purchase, but there was a very clear distinction between quality.

Let's look at other items that you may have in your kitchen that you may need to think about from time to time. The first is dishwashing liquid. Consider buying dishwashing liquid in bulk or spending a little extra on a better-quality product. Just as you did initially with decanting small amounts into a single unit. Use all of your dishwashing liquid before replacing it with a new one.

Replace drying towels on a regular basis even if you happen to have a dishwasher. You will always get to make use of washcloths and tea towels to keep surfaces neat and clean. These tea towels usually only have a limited lifespan so don't expect them to last forever without eventually losing their natural color or becoming stained by fats or cooking oil. Your best solution to this is to put them into the wash or soak immediately when you notice that they are looking that way. This will extend the life of those towels.

Store all chemical products high enough and out of reach in the event that you have small children or toddlers running around. They are naturally extremely curious and one of the last things you need is for them to ingest any of these substances. Be sure to keep each of these packed in the top of cupboards where only you can reach them. The best place for all of these products is in your laundry above where your washing machine and dryer are positioned. This is the ideal place for all your washing liquid, fabric softener cloths, dishwashing liquid, floor cleaning products, bleach, furniture polish, any cleaning products that may have harmful chemicals in.

Other items that can easily be stored above your washer and dryer are things like bulk toilet rolls.

Entrance Hall

Most homes in North America cater for fairly cool winters and entrance halls can become a nightmare when not kept clean. This can quickly become overrun with mud when it rains and plenty of sludge once it begins snowing. There are a couple of hacks to keep this area as clean as possible. Allowing you to possibly do a quick once over on a weekly basis rather than having to expend energy cleaning each and every day.

Depending on what your main entry point to your home is, whether you make use of the front door or you have an interlinking door between your garage and the main house, the key would be to place a mat directly outside where you're likely to enter. Use this mat to scrape off as much mud, dirt and grime as you possibly can. As you enter your home place a really simple seat close enough that you're able to sit down as soon as you enter.

Here you can undo your boots or footwear and ensure there are a couple of wicker baskets that have fabric inners that can be removed and easily thrown into the washer and dryer. This way you get all the footwear out of the way and you get to keep your entrance as neat and tidy as long as possible without having to do heavy cleaning daily during winter months.

If you have space in your entrance hall, a table could be an option where you can place a container for mail and another for keys. This will be ideal for remote controls for your garage doors and all those other items that you waste hours of valuable time looking for. If these containers happen to be there and it's one of the first things that you see when you walk into your home, eventually it will become second nature for you to drop all your essential things that you know you look for on a regular basis into the one basket.

The second basket should contain mail. This makes it easy to scroll through each envelope and decide what needs to be attended to immediately, what is unimportant, and what needs to be scheduled. All mail that is opened should be transferred to either a pinboard or the refrigerator door. It needs to be positioned somewhere that you get to notice it every day. That way you will never miss another important document again. Junk mail should be thrown out immediately, so it doesn't have a chance to gather.

A final essential item in your entrance hall is a coat holder and umbrella stand, or a rail for these items or an enclosed cupboard where these things can be stored. Firstly, this will free up valuable space in your living areas, but you have all the items that you really need at the entry and exit point of your home. You will never forget anything that you need on your way out ever again.

In the following chapter we will continue with things you need to consider when organizing your home by tidying and decluttering.

Chapter 4:

Scaling Down Continued...

"If one's life is simple, contentment has to come. Simplicity is extremely important for happiness. Having few desires, feeling satisfied with what you have, is very vital: satisfaction with just enough food, clothing, and shelter to protect yourself from the elements."
– The Dalai Lama, 1935

Moving into other areas of the home, let's focus on the dining area. In smaller homes the dining area is often used as a multipurpose room. There are usually computers or laptops and papers everywhere that indicate that work is being done. If you have school going children this is often where they complete tasks and assignments that need to be handed in. This is not the true purpose of a dining area and unless this is absolutely vital wherever possible try and make an alternative arrangement once you have moved furniture around and you can see what space you have available. In the meanwhile, keep this in the back of your mind.

Dining Room

The ideal dining area should be clean and clear with just your dining table and chairs, possibly a runner or cloth across the table, with a centerpiece in the form of a candle or a vase with fresh flowers. The only other furniture that belongs in a dining room is a sideboard where your entertainment dinner service, crockery and cutlery belong. In addition to this any specific table décor that you may use specifically when you are entertaining.

The sideboard is not the place for odds and ends, miscellaneous bits of paper or a storage spot for things that you have no idea where they belong. Depending on the size of your sideboard and what it looks like, the top should also be kept as neat and clutter free with minimal, clean lines. Keep things as simple as possible without overdoing décor.

Before adding your entertainment items to your sideboard unpack everything and review the same process with every item that you discover packed away. If things really have true meaning in your life then by all means, keep them somewhere safe until you know exactly where you think it can belong.

Bathrooms

There should be very little stored in bathrooms other than things like a toilet cleaner, toilet spray, hand soap, and possibly a hand cream. It can really make a difference if you decant the hand soap and hand cream into really nice-looking containers or be sure that the ones that you buy for use in your guest bathrooms and even your own bathroom are luxurious.

Bathrooms often have a closet built to hide plumbing beneath the basin, this often has shelving and is an excellent place to store extra toilet rolls, hand wash, toilet cleaner, hand cream, razor blades and shaving foam, keep all of these things out of sight and be sure that the only décor in the bathroom is possibly a healthy-looking plant that will thrive with the moisture, such as orchids, or a selection of rolled towels and face cloths in a suitable container.

One of the key focuses to bear in mind with this massive undertaking that you've decided to jump into is to keep areas as plain, simple, and neat as possible. A typical bathroom usually has soaps, shampoos, conditioners, razors, and shaving foam all over the bathroom, or around the bath. While this is what your bathroom may have looked like in the past, it's in the past and if you want to experience a much simpler lifestyle then you need to be able to simplify as much as possible. Hide all of the items you would normally find around a bath in the closet under the basin, or alternately, if you don't have a closet under the basin then it may be worthwhile buying a type of caddy with several drawers that can fit into the space available.

Make use of the drawers for each of the different items. One drawer can be specifically for toilet rolls, while another can hold shampoos and conditioners, or razors, shaving foam and body wash or soaps. Another drawer could contain a toilet cleaner. Extra toilet spray is a must, especially if this is a guest bathroom. The only things that should be visible in the bathroom should be towels, a healthy plant, soap in a dispenser and a moisturizing cream in a dispenser.

If you are making use of bath mats it's important that these should either be neutral in color, or they should blend in with the color of the towels. Subdued tones are better than going with bright colors unless they match the other accessories in the room.

Bedrooms

This is without a doubt where you will spend the most time sorting through things because most of the items in your bedroom will have sentimental value of some description or another. Remember that for this entire decluttering and reorganizing process to work, you need to be a willing participant, no matter how hard it gets trying to decide what to hang onto and what to let go.

Occasionally it's best to start with the very basics and work around there. How this will work is that you definitely need a bed. You need bedding to go on that bed. You need pillows or cushions. Notice that you are now looking at all the things that you specifically need, rather than the things that you may actually want, but you don't need.

Depending on what room you are sorting you may need bedside lamps or a lamp. Do you need a bedside table, or an upright chest of drawers? What other large items of furniture do you specifically need in the bedroom you're decluttering? If the answer to your question is nothing, then remove all other pieces of furniture. Even if you do this as a part-time exercise to see whether you are able to manage without the furnishings. If you have a TV in your bedroom is it on the TV cabinet? What else do you have on the TV stand? Does the TV stand have drawers or a closet section where you can place your CDs? Are there other items that are currently lying around that can be stored?

Let's continue working on the assumption that you are working with the master bedroom at the moment. This room may need a chest of drawers as well as built-in closets or a walk-in closet. You may want a single seater or a dresser if there's available space. For a master bedroom you will pretty much always need side tables. Whether these are attached to a headboard of some description or loose is a personal preference.

It's a good idea to go through these bedside closets on a regular basis to clear them of all excess papers and other items that you could be letting go of. Hanging onto clutter prevents positive energy from being able to flow freely around you. This is where it's believed that clutter can create mental barriers and has the potential to stifle our growth.

Next on the list would be bedroom closets. It's recommended that before you do this you sort out all your clothes into the five-pile system. You are probably going to find that you're prepared to get rid of a whole lot more than you originally bargained for.

If you live in areas that experience extreme winters then you probably already have your summer and winter wardrobes divided into separate places.

As you begin to sort clothing do everything all at once. That way you aren't going to have to come back to a major sort in a few months from now. Try and find some vacuum seal bags. These are perfect for storing clothing, bedding, curtains and a host of other things. They are reasonably priced for the amount of use you get out of them.

As you begin to sort your clothes into the different seasons, set aside those items that you want to keep and divide the balance between the other four piles. Whatever you do, don't go back and fetch an item from one of the other piles that you've already made a decision on. Trust your gut instinct, it's usually right.

Another yardstick for measuring whether something belongs in one of the other piles or not is how many times you have actually made use of that item, or happened to have worn it over the last 6-12 months? If your answer is zero, then it's time to say goodbye to that item no matter how fond you may have been of it.

With the items that are now remaining there are several things you can do to pack each garment in such a way that they're easy to find, easy to remove from your closet without disrupting what the entire closet looks like. Remember that the goal is not simply decluttering your space, it's also learning how to organize things in such a way that they are visually appealing rather than creating visual chaos.

Several ways to pack items such as jeans and trousers are by rolling them rather than folding them in thirds. Rolling them prevents them from creasing and also allows you to stack them vertically and horizontally on a shelf in a closet, maximizing the space that you have available to you.

There are many different ways to fold clothing to get the maximum benefit from them—consider how retailers fold their t-shirts and golf-shirts using a piece of cardboard. There are loads of videos on YouTube that can teach you how to fold anything from bulky jackets to socks efficiently. To keep your closet neat and tidy, think about securing some wicker baskets or even smaller plastic bins that can easily be pulled out of the closet whenever you are looking for something.

These same types of baskets can be used to hold socks, belts, ties and any number of smaller items. You may want to use baskets to hold things like hair dryers, hair straighteners that are currently lying around. The idea is that you make the most use of the space you have available to you.

You have probably experienced when you fold your trousers or t-shirts and place them in your closet neatly, only to have them looking disheveled and disorganized within a couple of days. It's almost impossible to move items around when they are stacked one on top of another without disrupting the entire system.

This is where the baskets or plastic containers come in. They are shallower, can be stacked one on top of another and by rolling your garments you can actually move and remove what you want without having to rearrange the entire closet.

If the wicker baskets have handles they can be inserted in the closet as if they were actual drawers. Whenever you needed something you could simply remove that basket, take it down, find what you need and return the basket without disrupting the entire closet.

Hanging Closets

Sorting through your hanging closets, arrange your clothes according to color and height. Place your longer jackets or dresses on one side of the closet with your shirts, trousers, or cardigans according to the same height. Next you are going to look at sorting all your shoes. The best way to work with shoes is either with a shoe rack, shoe boxes that can be stacked one on top of another, or simply stacking them in pairs. Once again work with height. On the shortest side of your clothes, stack your longest shoes, for example, if you have long boots, this is where they would go, underneath your blouses.

You are aiming at your shoes not becoming entangled with the clothes hanging in your cupboard. If your long boots are directly beneath your short blouses you can begin to scale your shoes down in height to match the length of the clothes in your closet. Where your longest skirts, dresses, trousers are, is where your flattest, lowest shoes should be.

Trunks and Additional Storage

The clothes that you have sorted to keep that may be for the opposite season to what you are now in should be folded as neatly as possible and placed in vacuum seal clothing bags. Once a bag is full, remove all of the excess oxygen from the bag. You will notice that the bag shrinks substantially and will now take up a fraction of the space it originally did. These vacuum sealed bags can possibly fit into the top of closets, or in additional storage spaces such as trunks or if you have underbed storage, this is exactly where each of these should go.

Using vacuum seal bags is not just as a space saving exercise, they protect your clothes from dust and water, insects, bugs, and other mites. These are also a potentially good investment if you have a fair number of items that you aren't entirely convinced that you're ready to part with just yet.

Trunks are great for storing all sorts of bits and bobs that don't really have a specific home just yet, but they hold too much sentimental value for you to want to get rid of them.

For the master bedroom and teens, you may often find deodorants that are not quite used up. Be sure to use everything and then instead of leaving empty containers lying around throw these out.

Children's Bedrooms

Repeat exactly the same process with any children's bedroom. The main difference between this and an adult room is that they grow out of their clothes a lot faster than adults do so be prepared for much larger piles of clothing, shoes, and other items to be given away.

The other thing that will need to be sorted when it comes to children are toys, books, and puzzles. This may take a fair amount of time. When it comes to puzzles be sure that all the pieces are there. If there are any pieces missing, throw it away. Psychologically you are wanting to teach your child how to perceive shapes and make connections. The lesson should not be one of frustration because there happens to be pieces of the puzzle missing.

The same goes for any toys that are broken. Sort these out and throw them away. In the chapters that follow we will be discussing ways to keep all of this clutter under control. Be sure to involve your child(ren) during this entire process so they learn what it's like to once again regain control over everything that takes control over their lives, much in the same way as we're affected as adults.

The examples we set for our children will be the ones they take with them into adulthood. This is one of the most important reasons for getting your own life back on track by decluttering and reorganizing your life.

Chapter 5:

The Decluttering Process

"Too many people spend money they haven't earned, to buy things they don't want, to impress people they don't like."
– Will Rogers

In this chapter we are going to discuss the process of being able to declutter and reorganize your home and possibly even your life. One of the first things to be cognizant of is that it's not how quickly you get there but rather getting there that makes the difference.

Small Steps Equal Giant Strides

Choosing to do a little at a time is better than making a decision to tackle an entire area only to lose interest within a couple of hours. It's much easier to set yourself a specific time limit, even if it's 30 minutes where you are going to then focus your effort entirely on completing one specific task. An example of this could be spending your first 30 minutes sorting through old papers, deciding what belongs in each of the five-piles. If you need to action anything then it needs to obviously be placed somewhere that it can easily be attended to.

In a previous chapter I referred to placing important documents that need your attention and action either on the refrigerator or on a pinboard in the kitchen. You may be wondering why the kitchen rather than a bedroom? The main reason is that you need to be able to rest and relax in your bedroom without having a constant visual reminder that becomes an open loop in your mind. You focus on it so intently that it's all that you think about.

Rather place this where you will definitely see it but you will also have the time, energy, and effort necessary to action whatever needs to be taken care of at the right time. See how much you can get done within a focused 30 minutes. You may just be pleasantly surprised by just how much you can do when you actually set your mind to it. Come the end of the 30 minutes you may find that you are now fully into the swing of things and you are now motivated to keep going.

Alternately you may feel that you are now sick of looking at paper and sorting them into different piles and you need to break your concentration after the allotted time. This is perfectly fine. Step back and take notice of exactly what you have accomplished during a dedicated amount of time. Scheduling 30-minute intervals to complete sorting and decluttering tasks may mean that the project takes longer than you may have originally anticipated but there is continuous forward motion. This forward momentum is all that you really need to allow a habit to form.

At the end of the first period, be sure that everything in the "throw away" pile is immediately thrown out. This should give you a visual sense of achievement being able to physically notice that what was once something that seemed an impossible task is finally being attended to. Even if you schedule 30 minutes each day, or 30 minutes every second day to work towards sorting, clearing out, cleaning, and making those major decisions whether you want to sell, or give away all the excess clutter you have lying around.

Investigate charity shops that may accept donations, these could be really great options when it comes to donating old clothing that is still in a good condition, many of them accept all sorts of items as long as they are still in working order. Do some research and look for those that are closest to you. Depending on the type of charity you would like to support, many of these charity shops operate in aid of animal shelters, for abandoned women, homeless shelters and so on. Spending a little time on the internet will help you identify where you can donate each of your items. Some of these institutions are even prepared to actually come and collect your donation from you.

As you begin getting into the meat of all your possessions and can gain a visual perspective of everything that you have, being completely objective about it you will surprise yourself with the sheer abundance and excess or duplicates that you have. By now you should have already recognized the value that comes with being able to liberate yourself of all the excess in exchange for something that's simpler and more manageable.

Be Realistic

Be realistic with your expectations from this project as well as from yourself. Don't take on more than you can reasonably handle at a time. This is possibly one of the biggest challenges that individuals face who are trying to make such drastic changes in their environments, their homes, and even in their lives. Allow yourself enough time to work your way through the parting process. For some this exercise can actually lead to further anxiety because you are now being separated from your possessions.

You are looking for ways to ultimately alter your lifestyle forever and not just for a band-aid to plaster over your clutter problem as a short-term solution. Don't ever lose sight of the first goal, which is to liberate yourself from as much of the excess that you are currently living with at the moment. It's being able to trim the cloth so to speak. This still doesn't mean that you aren't going to feel a bit of separation anxiety or look back and imagine what life would be like if you hadn't chosen to go this route. This takes us back to the very first chapter where you need to get your priorities and motivation in order before you can consider that you are feeling remorse over your decision.

Having all the clutter all around you was doing nothing to benefit you, in fact it was negatively influencing your mental health and possibly even your physical health. These two reasons, on their own present a valuable argument in support of this project and for you to follow through with your decluttering plan. What do we mean when we talk about a decluttering plan? This is simply an orderly "To do list" that has different steps and stages of what we have already discussed in each of the chapters above. It is writing each of these steps down so they become a visual reminder of a mental commitment you have made with yourself to improve your current living conditions and your lifestyle.

Take Time to Mourn

Allow yourself to rant, cry, miss your stuff, be tempted into buying new stuff to replace all the stuff you've just managed to get rid of (without following through of course). Once you feel you have managed to work through all of these emotions, return to the present moment. You should find that your mind will become that much clearer as to why you considered making such drastic changes to your life now.

A common thread that seems to be running through this entire chapter is acting on your intentions and physically doing the work to make it happen. Those who usually have the hardest time being separated from their possessions are those who are used to a particular lifestyle or status that owning all these nice things bring along with it.

Try and identify ways to make the transition from having everything that possibly opens and shuts, to paring that right down to just those things you need.

You may have bought many of your possessions as a way to keep up with the Joneses only to discover that their lifestyle is often fake and pretentious. When you realize this and know that that's not the type of individual you want to be, the way for you to complete this decluttering process will move forward and become successful. Know that there are going to be days when you feel negative and despondent.

Handling Your Emotions Professionally

When you're feeling overwhelmed it could be a sign that you're battling to deal with each of your emotions. Not only are having emotions important, but they are anticipated when you are making such a major transition in your home and in your life that's not only going to impact you but will have a knock-on effect with all the occupants of the home. Everyone needs to have bought into this decluttering project for it to be successful.

One of the best ways of dealing with the entire project when you're already feeling overwhelmed is to start with a simpler task and work your way through to the monumental task. Some of these spaces could include your garage, storage sheds that haven't been visited or sorted for some time could actually come across as being intimidating and add to those feelings of being overwhelmed.

There can be simple and workable solutions to dealing with one of these spaces:

Start with What You See

It's often easiest to deal with those things that are right in front of you that you can immediately see that you no longer want or need. Move these out the way or to a "ditch it, donate it, sell it" pile. Your brain should hardly even be registering what you are doing because it's all happening so quickly. Don't give it even a moment to stop you to question whatever you're holding in your hands.

The next step is to look at things that take up a lot of space. These are big items. Maybe it's a metal filing cabinet, or perhaps a boxing bag... maybe you have a set of mismatched golf clubs and haven't seen a golf course for at least the last five plus years. You're actually looking for items that look like they're out of place, damaged, or taking up a fair amount of space yet you hardly ever use it.

Remember that I mentioned in the chapters above that the moment you begin to physically see progress happening you will automatically feel inspired and motivated to continue on your decluttering journey.

By now you should have mastered the 30-minute sorting challenge and have that down pat. Take your large, unmanageable space and section it off into smaller pieces. As you move from section to section don't leave any section undone. Even if you are only completing a single section in a day. Remember that small habits equal great results. Set each of these smaller areas as stepping stones. That way you can celebrate once you have accomplished what you set out to achieve for the day. All these small victories add up to help make you feel positive about yourself.

In order to make your five-pile decision, you will need to actually hold each item you come across. Set a goal for yourself to only touch an item once. This is going to force you to make a decision regarding each of these items pretty quickly.

Set yourself a time limit for making that decision as well. This will often force you to go with your gut instinct which is a combination between heart and head. Your gut instinct is usually the correct decision. Remember the questions to ask yourself when the last time was that you actually made use of the item. If you cannot provide an accurate time frame that was within even the last 6-months, it's time for it to be added to the dump or donate piles.

Keep at it until you are sitting with more open spaces than you could have imagined. In the newly reorganized space, take each of those items you have considered worth keeping and find a suitable spot for each of these items. This will be their new home. Be sure that before you move anything into an altered environment, you have cleaned the area completely and be sure it is spotless.

Accept that this is going to take you time, effort, and plenty of energy.

What Prevents Us from Achieving Our Goals?

The same thing that usually prevents us from achieving all goals, fear, and negativity. We are often afraid that we are making the wrong decision when we choose to give up most of what we own to live a more simplified lifestyle.

We fear that by the time we've finished giving away most of our belongings we will be left with nothing. Dealing with fear can often be more challenging than you could ever imagine. Start off by cutting back on all those things that you have way too much of. You will have to deal with some pushback when it comes to identifying those items that need to be cut back. If you're sitting with tons of glasses but there are only two of you in a household, then you don't really need to sit with the massive abundance.

Reducing the number of things in your home will soon help you feel alive. You will feel invigorated because you'll be sitting with more available space than you could ever have imagined, and it will make you feel less stressed visually. Apart from this you will now be living in an environment that is clutter free that will make you feel as though slowly, but surely, you are making steady progress toward the major goal.

It's easy for procrastination to creep in while you're still in this phase. Don't even entertain it, this habit is trying to derail your entire journey. Keep going, there's no major rush to accomplish these goals, but you should set aside some goals and deadlines to make what you are doing be more authentic. You can choose to break these goals down into smaller milestones. This can be done either by considering one area completed as a milestone achieved, or everything being sorted when it comes to a single item, like all the paperwork. Setting goals up like the latter is often more difficult to quantify, than choosing to go the other route.

Reward Yourself

What's the point of reaching your goals and achieving everything you have set out to accomplish without a reward? Put it this way, you wouldn't normally work for an employer for nothing. As you achieve each of your benchmarks, reward yourself with something small, but meaningful to you. This could be something as simple as spending a couple of dollars at a Sushi Bar. Things to try and avoid as rewards are more materialistic things. Unless you are planning to follow the one-in and one-out philosophy which we will discuss in the following chapter.

Your ultimate goal in moving forward is toward a life that is simple and straight-forward. Remember right at the beginning I asked you to take a physical stocktake of everything that you happen to own, the reason for this is to show you exactly how much stuff you actually have. From this extensive list of items that could range from hats and handbags to skirts and snow skis, select five groups of items to begin working on immediately.

Once you have made inroads on these five items you can then consider the next five groups of items on your master list. As you deal with one lot of items take a black marker and draw a line through the item on the list. This provides you with another psychological boost for you to continue with this process.

Chapter 6:

Living with Less is Living More

> *"We go on multiplying our conveniences only to multiply our cares. We increase our possessions only to the enlargement of our anxieties."*
> *– Anna C. Brackett*

In this chapter we are going to look at many of the benefits that come with cutting back to your specific level of comfort while still being able to control the clutter around you.

Having Less Means Having a Lot Less:

Cleaning

Having less furniture and clutter makes cleaning a breeze. Rather than spending an entire day cleaning or every evening when you get back from work, you may now only need to do a quick once over once a week. Let's face it, it takes a very special person to thrive on cleaning all day long, even though we love the end result, getting there is simply the pits. Finally having a home that you can move around and maneuver around furniture, under couches, beds, chairs and so on, means a quick going over with a vacuum cleaner followed by a semi-dry mop and floor spray. Plush carpets can quickly be vacuumed without having to completely rearrange an entire room before being able to even turn the vacuum on.

Clean as You Go

Adopting this philosophy will sometimes take a while to get everyone on board with it but it becomes so much easier if everyone cleans up immediately after they have finished in bathrooms, brushing teeth, washing hands, bathing or taking showers, place dirty washing either in a linen bin immediately or see whether there is sufficient dirty washing to put a load on in the washing machine. Learning to clean up coffee or juice spills on kitchen counters or rinsing off chopping boards before stacking the dishwasher makes it easier for everyone because the work is not automatically left to one single individual.

Even small children and toddlers can be taught how to throw garbage in the bin, how to put their dirty clothes in the linen bin, and how to pick up toys, returning them to toy boxes or cupboards. They are never too young to be taught that making a contribution to the home is something that is normal. Older children can be given greater responsibility such as sorting things out for recycling, helping out with meal preparation and even learning how to cook on their own. They should also be able to load washing machines and dryers.

Debt

Your debt will be reduced proportionately because you won't be spending as much money on random items and running up your credit card debt. If you know anything about wise financial transactions then you will know how much money you are able to save simply by paying off a little extra each month on your mortgage account, credit cards and any debt linked to an interest rate that can fluctuate. By paying an extra couple of hundred dollars each month you can potentially shave years off your original loan amount. This alone sounds like cutting back will be a wise investment in your future.

Rearranging

You won't spend as much time rearranging your home because you will already have clean lines and simplified rooms with more open spaces to maneuver in. Should the rearranging bug bite you this will be done in a fraction of the time when you have limited furnishings in the space in question.

Stress

We've already discussed that clutter and too many possessions had the power to create large amounts of stress that manifest in each of us differently. Without excess clutter these stress levels are actually reversed and the happy hormones and endorphins are released. The more stuff we had the more likely we were to stress about it, whether it was safe and secure, whether it was suitably covered in the event of some catastrophe. By scaling down on possessions, insurance rates could be decreased accordingly, leaving you slightly better off financially each month.

Greater Financial Freedom

Financial Freedom ties in with being in control of your financial situation rather than your finances dictating terms to you. It's a pretty great feeling having additional money over at the end of each month that could either be invested or used to pay off debts with financial institutions.

Increased Energy

Clutter, chaos, and disorganization was able to drain almost every ounce of energy out of you. Now that you are back in control of your own environment, you will potentially have an increased amount of energy to direct into working to improve your current environment.

Increased energy assists you to get things done that need to be done when they need to be done.

Following are a number of life hacks to help you with your decluttering and organizing experience:

Assess Your Home as a Visitor

Once you have made all the changes to simplifying your home, enter and evaluate your home as if you were a stranger visiting for the first time. Take notes as you view the reorganized and simplified spaces with a critical eye. If there are more things that need to be moved, toned down, or possibly even accentuated, then make these changes as part of the holistic process.

Take Some Before and After Photographs

Consider taking several before and after photographs of the space you are looking at working in. This can be especially effective for smaller spaces such as bathrooms, laundry's, entrance halls, and even parts of bedrooms. You may just be pleasantly surprised at the major transformation that has already taken place.

Take up a 10 – 10 – 10 Challenge

Look for 10 x items you are willing to throw away, 10 x items you are willing to give away, and 10 x items need to find the right home for. By home I mean the perfect spot for it within your home. Repeat this same challenge on a regular basis. This will prevent you from accumulating more of the same.

Donate Clothing You no Longer Wear

Clothing that is still in a good condition can be donated to Goodwill or given to those who are homeless and may be able to make use of them. It's vitally important that these clothing items aren't torn or stained or in a condition where you wouldn't feel comfortable wearing these items yourself. Discard all clothing that is broken or damaged and cannot be repaired.

Enlist the Help of Others

Get some of your closest friends or family members involved with this project. Ask them to be specifically tough on you when it comes to arguing to keep items. If your negotiation skills aren't up to standard and you aren't able to convince them otherwise, the item should be placed in the 'undecided' pile.

Fill a Trash Bag for Goodwill

See how quickly you can try and fill a trash bag with items you're happy to donate to goodwill. These can be anything from ornaments, clothing, shoes, handbags, and anything in between.

Just One Item Daily

This is a very interesting but powerful concept of how small things can compound to become great over an extended time. Look for just one item to give away each day. Imagine that by the end of the year you have already managed to make a dent in the things that you own by parting with 365 items. By the end of the second year... You get the picture! Very powerful habit to be able to embrace and build on.

Start Off Small

The above is a perfect example of doing something small every single day that's going to make a huge difference by the end of a 12-month period. You won't necessarily see or feel the change instantly, but if you are keeping accurate records of your decluttering journey you will discover exactly what you've been able to rehouse with someone who really needs it more than you do.

Work According to a To Do List

Instead of working randomly, draw up a to do list that has actionable points that you can follow and then mark off once each item has been done. The plan is for you to be able to visually see progress taking place each day as you're able to strike out actions that you've been able to complete. The more lines you have crossed out the closer you are to experiencing your declutter and organizing journey.

Stick with It

Tenacity is a skill or characteristic that not everyone has. Once you commit to making this lifestyle change you need to be prepared to see it through to the end. This includes seeing it as something that is only going to benefit you and your family, your home, your mental health, as well as your physical health. Whenever you feel tempted to give it all up, remember to stick with it. Imagine all the benefits once you reach the point where change is visible.

Make This an On-going Habit

Getting into the on-going habit of making these lifestyle changes will benefit your life and the lives of your children, potentially for generations. There is currently so much consumerism in the world today and we are influenced wherever we look, whether these are billboards on the side of the road, adverts appearing across social media, one of the greatest gifts you can give your children is the choice to live in the kind of world that is dictated to by the rest of the world or whether they are going to plan their futures for themselves.

Keeping Clutter Under Control

One of the major ways of keeping clutter under control is something referred to as a "one-for-one." The best way to explain this is that for every new item you want to introduce into your home (irrespective of what it is), needs to happen on a sacrificial basis. To add something to the home you must decide on something that needs to go. An example of this could be that you're considering adding another pair of jeans to your existing wardrobe. Before you can do this, you need to either find another pair of jeans that you're prepared to give away, throw away, or donate. This will always ensure that you keep sticking with the same sorts of numbers of items at any given time.

You want to replace or purchase new towels for your bathrooms, find an old set of towels that you're prepared to part with. This way your equilibrium remains constant. Make sense? Excellent! Let's move onto systems.

Set Up Your Systems.

Whenever you come across this expression what are some of the first words that spring to mind? For me it is making certain that whatever I am currently doing to declutter and keep my home organized and in the very best possible condition, I am going to have to be completely ruthless at times, especially when it comes to learning to let things go. Something important under this heading is that the system that you implement should be the one that works specifically for you.

You may definitely find help and other information online, but you will need to establish your own rules of engagement that will meet your own specific needs, rather than playing to someone else's rules. Stick with the basics and you are sure to win at the end of the day. If you are part of a cohesive family unit, one of the first things is to ensure you have everyone's buy-in that they are going to support you and assist you. Discover what their main motivation is for each wanting to be living in a neater, more organized, decluttered space. Their motivation can quite possibly be completely different from the one that you have and that's perfectly okay.

Refine Over Time and Streamline Even Further

Your constant progress over time could very well change as this becomes a habit for you. You may find that certain things work for you, while something we've recommended in these chapters doesn't necessarily resonate with you. Remember that each move that you make should be something to motivate you and move you towards being able to declutter all the spaces around you. It's all about finding your own way of doing things that work for you. Maybe you are happy working with a three-pile system rather than having to go back through things in an 'undecided' pile. Many of your habits can be adapted and modified or streamlined as you go. Find what works best for you and stick to that or make the necessary changes as you get there. There's no use following somebody else's method unless it makes perfectly good sense to you. All that this will do will be to frustrate you and maybe even keep you from completing this exercise at least once. I am not going to even try and convince you that this process is going to be one that is easy. It will be well worth it however once you begin to see results, once you no longer have to waste precious time that can be wisely invested doing those things that are important and really matter to you. You may find that you need to fine-tune and tweak some of the processes we have identified here. This is perfectly fine, you do whatever works well for you.

Slow and Steady Progress

No matter how slow you go, don't stop moving forward. Keep a constant motion going as this will be a sure way for you to avoid procrastination. The adage that "procrastination is the thief of time" is something that is so true. The longer you wait, deliberate, or procrastinate in getting the job done, the longer it is going to be before you can truly begin to enjoy not only your home and the space surrounding it, but also beginning to relax and enjoy your life. It's saying, "no to consumerism" and taking control over your spending habits and discovering new and exciting ways to spend your free time rather than wasting it constantly cleaning clutter, or cleaning around the clutter.

Procrastination

When it comes to procrastination, try and implement something that is recommended by productivity expert David Allen in his bestselling book, *Getting Things Done*... He confirms that the brain only has the mental capacity to focus on about four things at any given time. So, make these four things count. The point that I'd like to make regarding his formula for getting things done—is to "touch it once." This is not always practical, especially if you are trying to get a 'vibe' going to determine whether you want to keep something, or you're prepared to part with it.

This may mean actually physically holding something to decide whether you can live without it or not. I would recommend that you don't spend too much time on this process because it could possibly derail you and waste even more of your precious time. Try this method of holding something to determine whether it is something you want to keep or not. Once you've made your decision, then set the item aside and leave it as that.

Make a firm decision that you aren't going to go back to fetch it out of the box, bin or garbage bag. Be firm on yourself and once you have made a decision stick with it. It is really going to be the only way you will ever be able to move through this process successfully.

Keeping Motivated

Try and find ways to keep yourself motivated throughout your project. This can be challenging at times and you may even feel as though you are marking time on the spot. There may be days when you simply cannot see any progress being made at all. This can especially be true when it comes to the very beginning stages and you're sorting through mountains of paperwork that we all seem to accumulate and want to hang onto forever.

This is where the friends or family members whose help you've enlisted are also able to come to the party. Be as honest and open with them as you can be throughout your dialogue. Explain to them that you are battling with motivation and let them help you with encouragement. You might want to even mention this to them at the beginning stages when you ask them to support you or help you.

Tell them that there are going to be times where, following through and pushing the envelope is going to be hard going. There's nothing quite like a positive support structure. Let them check in with you regularly—or you check in with them to let them know how things are going. There's no point in requesting assistance from these individuals unless you are actually going to accept it and use it to your full advantage. Rely on their comments and encouragement to help you achieve your goals. Once you've done so, remember to celebrate your victory along with them.

Repurposing Storage Containers

Several things you will need as you begin to sort out all your possessions are containers, boxes, drawers, baskets, caddy's and so on. One of the best and easiest ways of getting this right is by repurposing things that you already have lying around the home. Why is this so important? Well, you are essentially killing two birds with one stone. You are managing to find a use for items you already have in your home, that can be used effectively for something else. Be sure that whatever you are going to repurpose is strong and stable enough to be able to withstand those things that you have ideally identified them for.

An example of this would be for you to avoid placing a cardboard container in a bathroom where there is a lot of moisture. This doesn't matter how good it looks there, find something that ideally belongs there. In previous chapters we have spoken of repurposing glass jars. Consider this as an option for things like cotton balls, Q-tips, and possibly tissues. Something that I have seen in a bathroom that made perfect sense was a large set of plastic drawers. Each drawer was semi-transparent and contained different things that could be used in the bathroom. Because this was a small bathroom it made sense that this caddy was stacked as high as possible, each drawer was labeled with what was inside, making it easy to find whatever they were looking for. The only challenge I could see with a caddy like this is having to be exceptionally disciplined to ensure that what was labeled on the outside of the drawer was actually what was in the drawer itself. In this bathroom, the husband and wife had split a certain number of drawers for his grooming products, with the balance going to her.

Persevere Through the Pain

Nobody is promising that this entire process will be an easy one because it's going to bring its own set of challenges. There will be times when you will be totally torn between what you want to let go of and what you want to keep. Remember that this process is for you in the long run. It's helping you to reduce the amount of clutter surrounding you everywhere you look. Getting to the point where you are mentally and physically exhausted because you just have such an abundance of belongings, there is no time like the present to keep you motivated and for you to be able to persevere through the pain of making each and every change necessary.

In this final chapter we have covered many of the challenges and benefits of making the decision to follow through with decluttering your space. Remember to rely on those around you and enjoy the journey. It will certainly be more than worth it.

Conclusion

"Be content with what you have; rejoice in the way things are. When you realize there is nothing lacking, the whole world belongs to you."
– Lao Tzu

Throughout each of the chapters we have looked at specific ideas that you can easily implement immediately to make your home the environment of your dreams. We've considered some of the best ways to find a single starting point within your home, but only once you have come to a firm commitment that this is something you really want to do and being able to identify your reasoning behind your decision.

This reason will often be referred back to especially during those tough times when you feel like quitting or when things become challenging. Remember that you are not only doing this to minimize all the clutter and chaos around you, but you are possibly looking at ways to scale down without having to feel as though you will be deprived of any of your normal creature comforts. As we have moved throughout almost every room in the home you can get a better understanding of some of the areas that need to carefully be considered to neaten up, tidy the overall look or functionality of the space available to you.

By the end of the entire decluttering process you will more than likely want to move the space once more so the energy in the home is able to flow freely. You should be able to feel those areas in the home where there is still too much stuff. Part of what you are trying to achieve is balance and harmony. Once you manage to accomplish each of these, the rest is being able to add accents that add touches of your own specific personality to your space.

That's the secret—it's your space and you and your family need to be comfortable living in it. Life is worth living after all. For some individuals, cutting everything right down to the bare bones is their idea of decluttering and becoming totally organized, while for others it means being able to simplify, declutter and reorganize those things that you already have without parting with too much.

Whatever works best for you, your home. And your family should be the option chosen here. It really doesn't matter whether minimalism is currently a fashionable trend or not. Most individuals that go through this massive transition in their lives are looking for major change. They are tired of the constant pressure of having to face cleaning every other day, weekends, and spending most holidays doing heavy cleaning work.

This is not for just one member of the family. Without everyone's buy-in you will never be able to accomplish the goals that you have envisioned for your home. You will constantly be fighting an uphill battle when it comes to trying to minimize possessions, to making large changes that could shift the dynamics in your home. This is why it's so important for everyone to become actively engaged in as much of the process and the work as possible.

Remember that making a decision based on what you really want to keep should ideally be all those things that usually bring you and those around you joy and happiness.

Be prepared to face obstacles and challenges, as well as procrastination lulls that threaten to bring your entire project to a screeching halt... Accept that this is part of the process and you can move past it. Even if you need to slow things down a little or take a breather between your declutter effort. Rather spend even 5 minutes daily working on a small area than trying to complete sorting the entire garage within an hour.

Remember that this is not a race to get to the finish line first, no matter how desperate you are to see your home sorted out and complete. There's no rapid-fire solution to getting this done. Be realistic. In most instances if you've been living in the same space for more than a couple of years you have already accumulated way more than you need. Making big, bold, decisions in a hurry is not always the best way to go.

Choose the smallest space first and don't move on to another section until you are 100% satisfied with the end result. Once you've been able to stick to your to do list and you remain satisfied with the outcome of each of the rooms that you're working with, you will begin to feel excited and motivated to do more.

Enjoy the journey toward a less cluttered lifestyle. Enjoy the time with your family in an environment that no longer needs so much attention. Enjoy the satisfaction of knowing that if you really apply yourself you can accomplish anything. Whenever you are battling with any of the pointers I've shared with you, go back to the chapters in question to either receive some more motivation or to discover what you may need to do differently to achieve a different result.

It is my sincere wish that you find your decluttering and organizing experience one that is cathartic, one that allows you to grow, and live in a beautiful home that is free of all the stuff that we accumulate over the years. Instead, surround yourself with those things that add joy to your world and your life.

As an author I am constantly working towards improving as an individual as well as presenting you, the reader with quality, informative content. If you have enjoyed this book, please feel free to leave a note in the comments section. I do make myself available to read each and every one of these.

Printed in Great Britain
by Amazon